The Rise and Fall of American Growth

American Growth

The U.S. Standard of Living Since the Civil War

by Robert J. Gordon

Instaread

Please Note

This is a summary with analysis.

Table of Contents

Overview

The Rise and Fall of American Growth is an analysis of American growth from 1870 to the present. It focuses especially on the unprecedented "special century" of 1870-1970.

Throughout most of human history, economic growth was basically flat or advanced very slowly. After the Civil War in the United States, however, life began to improve exponentially. This was due to a series of "Great Inventions," including, most notably, electricity, the means of channeling and directing electricity, and the internal combustion engine. Homes became tied to systems of electricity, heat, and sewage. The last was particularly important, as cleaner water, abetted by new medicines that immunized against childhood disease, led to a dramatic drop in infant and child mortality.

The progress between 1870 and 1970 is routinely underestimated by measures of gross domestic product (GDP) because GDP does not measure the quality of life improvement by increased life expectancy. GDP also does not adequately measure the improvement in job conditions as new technology meant that men shifted from physical labor on the farm to less grueling jobs. Women no longer had to spend their days hauling water into the home and could begin to join the workforce.

After 1970, progress slowed. The Great Inventions could only be invented once. Once electricity, automobiles, and running water were widely available, they could not be developed and made widely available again.

The one area of continued progress since 1970 has been in communications technology. The development of desktop computers, the Internet, search engines, and cell phones contributed to a modest upswing in growth in 1994-2004. However, advances in communications cannot transform society in the way that the inventions of the special century did.

Future growth in the United States faces a number of obstacles. Rising inequality, an aging population, an underperforming educational system, and the breakup of the American family have slowed growth. Even if these problems are addressed, however, growth is unlikely to return to the level of the special century. The United States needs to take steps to improve the welfare of its citizens while recognizing that the miraculous growth rates of the special century cannot be repeated.

Important People

Robert J. Gordon is a professor of economics at Northwestern University. In addition to *The Rise and Fall of American Growth*, he has written a number of other books including *Macroeconomics* (2002) and *The Measurement of Durable Good Prices* (1990).

Henry Ford (1863-1947) was an industrialist best known for standardizing the production of the early automobile, thereby making cars widely available and affordable.

Thomas Edison (1847-1931) was an American inventor who created the first commercially viable, long-lasting electric light bulb.

Karl Benz (1844-1929) was a German inventor credited with developing the first internal combustion engine for the automobile.

Alexander Graham Bell (1847-1922) was an American inventor who patented the first telephone.

Robert M. Solow is a Nobel Prize-winning economist who is famous for isolating the amount of growth attributable to technical progress.

Key Takeaways

1. Great inventions can only be invented once. Growth associated with those inventions is therefore unique and cannot be duplicated.

2. Measures of GDP greatly understate the growth and impact of the great inventions on people's lives during the special century.

3. It can take many decades for inventions to have their full impact on growth via secondary inventions and improvements.

4. The linking of homes to heating, electrical, and sewage systems was one of the central advances of the special century, and was particularly important to increases in life expectancy.

5. The Great Depression and World War II helped fuel growth.

6. Technological improvements in telecommunications and entertainment from the 1990s through the 2010s cannot transform society as did the great inventions of the special century.

7. The United States faces major obstacles to growth, including inequality, aging demographics, and educational underachievement.

8. Even if the United States overcomes obstacles to growth, the country will not return to the growth rates of the special century.

Thank you for purchasing this Instaread book

**Download the Instaread mobile app to get
unlimited text & audio summaries
of bestselling books.**

Visit Instaread.co
to learn more.

Analysis

Key Takeaway 1

Great inventions can only be invented once. Growth associated with those inventions is therefore unique and cannot be duplicated.

Analysis

Thomas Edison developed a functional, long-lasting electric light bulb in October 1879. Ten weeks later, Karl Benz developed a workable internal combustion engine. These two inventions transformed life in the United States over the next century. Homes that had once been dark could now be lit. Similarly, the car made long-distance travel convenient and easy and ended reliance on horses, with their inefficiencies and vast quantities of manure.

Electricity and automobiles created the modern world. But that modern world could only be created once. The same can be said of other developments, such as working sewage systems, or penicillin, or the Internet. Inventions can spur fantastic growth, and this growth can last for some time. But inventions do not result in continuous growth. Once their impact has been absorbed, only new inventions can lead to new growth.

One way to think about the one-time-only nature of the great inventions of the past is to try to imagine what it would take to spur a similar technological revolution in the 2010s. Elaborations on earlier inventions, such as driverless cars, would result in minor alterations in people's lives, but not in wholesale transformations as the great inventions did.

Science fiction is filled with imagined inventions that could be as transformative as the great inventions of 1870-1970. For instance, if someone developed the kind of teleportation technology described in *Star Trek* and other works of science fiction, standards of living and everyday life could change drastically. At first, there might just be a large drop in the price of goods and materials as shipping costs disappeared. Over time, as the technology became more efficient and portable, public transportation and cars could disappear. Cities could be transformed; travel around the globe would be instantaneous, rearranging and reinventing entire industries. Even buildings might change in structure; they might no longer need doors or entryways.

Once the teleportation revolution happened, though, it could not happen again. Teleportation would cause massive growth and unpredictable, perhaps unimaginable, changes in every area of people's lives. But the changes would be unique; they would not generate growth forever.

Instead, for there to be more growth, there would need to be more inventions—in nanotechnology, perhaps, or bioengineering.

Key Takeaway 2

Measures of GDP greatly understate the growth and impact on people's lives during the special century.

Analysis

Official rates of growth of GDP during the years 1870-1970 are high, but they do not capture the full extent of growth during this period. GDP measures only goods and services exchanged. It does not measure other improvements in quality of life.

For instance, before 1870, farmers had to do back-breaking work in the fields by hand. By 1970, farmers had access to tractors and machinery that made the job vastly less physically demanding. GDP figures do not capture these quality of life changes.

Between 1870 and 1940, GDP per capita tripled, from about $2,800 per person to about $9,600 per person. But researchers have suggested that improvements in infant mortality rates alone mean that GDP may understate quality of life improvements over this period by from 50 to 100 percent.

Since GDP fails to capture many of the most important measures of quality of life, economists have been working to try to develop new metrics. One of these is the Social Progress Index, developed by Michael Green, executive director of the Social Progress Imperative. [1] The SPI uses more than 50 social and environmental indicators. In 2015, the United States, China, and Japan had the three highest GDP per capita ratings. [2] But Norway, Sweden and Switzerland led the way in SPI based on factors such as access to shelter, treatment of the environment, and access to higher education. [3]

Focusing on factors such as those in the SPI provides a much fuller picture of the advances in the special century than merely looking at GDP. SPI includes factors such as access to electricity, access to sanitary water, and life expectancy—all of which improved dramatically during the special century, and all of which are captured, at best, indirectly in measures of GDP.

Key Takeaway 3

It can take many decades for inventions to have their full impact on growth via secondary inventions and improvements.

Analysis

The internal combustion engine was developed in 1879. However, the transformation of transportation took many more years to complete. Horse-drawn vehicles remained the norm in cities until 1905. Henry Ford began mass-producing his Model T in 1908, putting cars within reach of a broad American public. By 1917, horse-drawn vehicles were largely gone in cities, though it took another three decades before mechanized tractors replaced horses on farms.

Important inventions do not cause immediate economic growth and improvement for everyone. Rather, they must be adapted and disseminated over time, a process that can result in steady growth over a surprisingly long period of time.

If inventions take a while to have their full effect, it follows that the immediate future of growth depends on inventions that have already been developed. If a transformative technology has been developed in 2015, then one can predict that growth for several decades—perhaps through 2035, perhaps for even longer—will be substantial.

As of 2014, however, no transformative technology seems to have been developed. Lists of current inventions instead focus on smaller-scale advances. For example, a CNBC list of inventions that could change the world includes a self-cleaning water pipe, self-driving cars, a portable dialysis machine, and a robotic arm that could make deliveries easier. [4] All of these inventions would certainly improve life for some individuals. But none has the potential to alter the entire landscape of cities or revolutionize farming the way the internal combustion engine did. A robot arm has little potential to generate decades of secondary improvements and changes.

Key Takeaway 4

The linking of homes to heating, electrical, and sewage systems was one of the central advances of the special century, and was particularly important to increases in life expectancy.

Analysis

Before 1870, houses were stand-alone, isolated structures. By 1940, they had been connected to five important systems: electricity, water, gas, telephone, and, perhaps most important of all, sewage.

The connection of homes to these systems transformed daily life in many ways. Homes were no longer frigid and dark in the winter. For women, electricity automated many household tasks such as washing clothes and cleaning dishes. Water connections meant that women no longer spent a huge portion of their day hauling water into the home.

Perhaps the most important result of these systems was an increase in life expectancy. The decrease in infant mortality and increase in life expectancy are often attributed to advances in medicine, such as penicillin. However, researchers have found that medical advances really had only a negligible effect of about 3.5 percent on life expectancy. The most important factor reducing infant mortality was clean water and better sanitation, which together are perhaps the greatest preserver of life in the history of the United States.

The 2016 water crisis in Flint, Michigan, emphasizes how health depends not just on modern medicine but on modern utility systems. In Flint, Michigan Governor Rick Snyder and various regulatory agencies engaged in cost-cutting measures to save money in the state budget. [5] As a result of their negligence, the water in Flint became contaminated with lead and other dangerous chemicals. People who drank the water developed rashes and hair loss. There was also an outbreak of Legionnaire's disease—a serious form of bacterial pneumonia that can result in death. [6]

After the water was declared unsafe, Flint residents faced further hardships. They could not drink, wash, or brush their teeth with water from their taps. Instead, they had to acquire bottled water for all their needs. People were essentially returned to pre-1870 conditions, when all water had to be hauled into the house. [7]

Key Takeaway 5

The Great Depression and World War II helped fuel growth.

Analysis

Growth in the special century was especially impressive between 1920 and 1970. This is because of the combined effects of the Great Depression and World War II. Generally, the Great Depression is seen as a time when growth stalled and reversed. In fact, legislation promoting unionization during the Depression increased wages, leading to investment in capital. Shorter work hours also lowered fatigue and increased efficiency. These gains were expanded during World War II, when massive government investment in manufacturing created a powerful boost in technology and capacity.

If large-scale wartime expenditure and investment had such a powerful effect on the economy, why hasn't government engaged in similar expenditures during peacetime in an effort to end recessions or jump-start economic activity? The main reason is probably ideological. [8] Businesspeople in peacetime are often concerned that large-scale government intervention will interfere with their businesses and freedom. Government spending also requires government revenues; absent the necessity of war, many people resent higher taxes. World War II helped fuel growth by reorganizing the entire economy. The war also required real sacrifices; rationing was required to maximize resource allocation, which improved manufacturing efficiency at the cost of civilian discomfort. In peacetime, without a major crisis, people, businesses, and government itself are not likely to want to make such sweeping changes.

Key Takeaway 6

Technological improvements in telecommunications and entertainment from the 1990s through the 2010s cannot transform society as did the Great Inventions of the special century.

Analysis

The development of the Internet, search engines, VCRs, DVDs, and other technologies helped create a growth surge between 1994 and 2004. However, this surge was much smaller and less sustained than the growth during the special century. That is because advances in communications are much more limited in effect than changes caused by electricity, the internal combustion engine, the networked home, and medical advances. For example, changes in communication technology are unlikely to have large-scale effects on life expectancy.

Some techno-optimists argue that advances in communications and computers could revolutionize all aspects of life. If scientists create real artificial intelligence (AI), they argue, computer intelligence will be smarter than humans. It will then be able to create unimaginable advances. Optimists refer to this as the Singularity: the moment when AI creates a cascade of innovations, changing life on earth forever. [9]

The special century could be seen as having the effect anticipated for the Singularity; technological change transformed the world in unimaginable ways. Will AI lead to another such revolution? There is little evidence that it will at any time in the foreseeable future. At the moment, innovations in computers, cell phones, and robotics are nowhere near as sweeping in implication or effect as Edison's light bulb. As a result, the big technological transformations are behind the United States, not ahead of it.

Key Takeaway 7

The United States faces major obstacles to growth, including inequality, aging demographics, and educational underachievement.

Analysis

Many factors have retarded growth since the 1970s. One of the most important is rising inequality. During 1917 to 1948, the gap between the wealthiest and poorest Americans decreased. Since 1970, that pattern reversed, as the top 10 percent of income earners pulled away from the bottom 90 percent. In 2013, income for the bottom 90 percent was lower than it had been in 1973, even as the income of the top 10 percent almost doubled. This means that real growth for most in the United States is overstated by GDP per capita figures.

Another obstacle to growth is demographic. Low birth rates and an aging population mean that more people in the United States are retiring, which means less productivity and a strain on pension systems. Rising costs and growing inequality have also caused college graduation rates to stagnate.

One possible way to address both inequality and graduation rates is free college. Government-subsidized free college was proposed by a 2016 contender for the Democratic presidential nomination, Bernie Sanders. His plan, which would cost about $70 billion, proposed making tuition and fees free at all public universities. The plan would be paid for by a tax on stock deals. [10]

Students often have trouble completing college because of high debt burdens and the need to work; free college would reduce these problems and allow more students to graduate. Free tuition would also make college affordable to low-income people, offering them access to training and higher paying jobs. Taxing the wealthy to fund free college tuition for all is a way to move money from the top 10 percent to the bottom 90 percent, thereby decreasing economic inequality.

Key Takeaway 8

Even if the United States overcomes obstacles to growth, the country will not return to the growth rates of the special century.

Analysis

Overcoming some of the obstacles to growth could help spread growth more equally and perhaps give a mild nudge to overall growth. However, growth rates in the near future are unlikely to be robust, and certainly will not approach those of the special century. This is not a comment on the failure of the US economic system. Rather, it affirms the unusual achievement of the special century. Through most of history, slow or zero growth was the norm. The fact that the United States has returned to more normal, slower growth should not distract from what it has achieved.

If the United States really is facing an extended period of very moderate growth, then there are serious political consequences. Both Democrats and Republicans tend to focus on economic growth as a solution to problems of poverty, medical care, and insufficient resources in any number of areas. When people do not have enough food or medicine, or cannot afford homes, politicians argue that the United States requires more economic growth.

If no growth is coming, though, then the United States will need to turn to different solutions. Rather than looking to growth, those in need will have to be helped using current resources. This will require difficult decisions about taxation and spending. And it would require different kinds of conversations about future plans and policies; conversations that do not depend on the miracle of special-century-like growth to address US failings.

Author's Style

Robert J. Gordon's writing is clear and direct, and he provides a remarkable level of detail about everyday life. Information about the volume of horse manure emitted in cities before the invention of cars is particularly vivid. There are also numerous statistics and charts, and many technical discussions about growth measurement. The book is aimed at economists as much as it is aimed at a general audience.

The Rise and Fall of American Growth is also significantly longer than it needs to be. Gordon's book is not intended to be gripping. Rather, he intends to present an argument that challenges assumptions about limitless American growth. Anticipating his critics, he clearly states his main points, offers evidence, and repeats his claims. This rhetorical strategy facilitates skimming, as his chapter conclusions in many cases recapitulate the entire chapter's arguments.

Author's Perspective

Robert J. Gordon is an economics professor. Before *The Rise and Fall of American Growth*, he wrote books such as his 1990 text *The Measurement of Durable Good Prices*—not a subject likely to hit the best-seller lists. His approach is unapologetically wonky. He makes lengthy detours to discuss academic economic arguments about the best way to measure GDP.

Gordon's wonkishness makes it difficult to pin down his political leanings or preferences. He has some sympathy for the work of Charles Murray, a conservative political scientist who warns about the dangers of the breakdown of the traditional family. But he also argues for many liberal policy positions, such as higher tax rates on the wealthy.

Ultimately, Gordon's perspective is one that is likely to irritate both the left and right. Conservatives argue that reducing regulation and cutting taxes will spur growth. Liberals argue that reducing inequality and investing in education will generate growth. Gordon says, on the contrary, that nothing either liberals or conservatives do is likely to return the United States to the growth rates of the 1960s.

Thank you for purchasing this Instaread book

**Download the Instaread mobile app to get
unlimited text & audio summaries
of bestselling books.**

Visit Instaread.co
to learn more.

References

1. Keohane, Georgia Levenson. "GDP Is a Bad Measure of Our Economy—Here's a Good One." *Time*, April 19, 2015. Accessed March 30, 2016. http://time.com/3826731/is-gdp-dead/

2. Knoema. "World GDP Ranking 2015: Data and Charts." Accessed March 30, 2016. http://knoema.com/nwnfkne/world-gdp-ranking-2015-data-and-charts

3. Social Progress Imperative. "Social Progress Index 2015." Accessed March 30, 2016. http://www.socialprogressimperative.org/data/spi#data_table/countries/spi/dim1,dim2,dim3

4. CNBC. "11 inventions that could change the world." June 11, 2014. Accessed March 30, 2016. http://www.cnbc.com/2014/06/11/11-inventions-that-could-change-the-world.html?slide=1

5. Graham, David A. "Who Is to Blame for Flint's Water Crisis?" *The Atlantic*, March 24, 2016. Accessed March 30, 2016. http://www.theatlantic.com/politics/archive/2016/03/flint-task-force-rick-snyder-blame/475182/

6. Ibid.

7. Palmer, Gianna. "Flint water crisis: Living one bottle of water at a time." *BBC News*, January

22, 2016. Accessed March 30, 2016. http://
www.bbc.com/news/magazine-35376517

8. Goodwin, Doris. "The Way We Won: America's
Economic Breakthrough During World War II."
American Prospect (Fall 1992). Accessed March
30, 2016. http://prospect.org/article/way-we-
won-americas-economic-breakthrough-during-
world-war-ii

9. Newitz, Annalee. "What Is The Singularity And
Will You Live To See It?" *Io9*, May 10, 2010.
Accessed March 31, 2016. http://io9.gizmodo.
com/5534848/what-is-the-singularity-and-
will-you-live-to-see-it

10. Desiderio, Andrew. "Sanders Unveils Tuition-
Free College Plan." *Real Clear Politics*, May 22,
2015. Accessed March 31, 2016. http://www.
realclearpolitics.com/articles/2015/05/22/
sanders_unveils_tuition-free_college_plan.
html

CPSIA information can be obtained
at www.ICGtesting.com
Printed in the USA
LVOW04s1447061016
507697LV00014B/589/P